Cuisinart Multi-Cooker Cookbook for Beginners

1000-Day Amazingly Easy & Delicious Cuisinart Multi-Cooker Recipes to Sauté Vegetables, Brown Meats and Slow Cook Your Favorite Comfort Foods for Busy People

Fiech Shems

Table of Contents

Introduction

This cookbook includes detailed information on how to cook every single recipe to a perfect point. This includes the methods, timings and quantities. Any tips and tricks required to make your recipes perfect and displayed in this cookbook, and you will be very soon be able to reach all your cooking skills potential. Now it's time to start cooking and stop worrying!

Cuisinart Multi-Cooker Cookbook will guide you step by step on how to use it to create fantastic recipes to Sauté Vegetables, Brown Meats and Slow Cook Your Favorite Comfort Foods for Busy People. Detailed calorie and macro-nutrients information has been included to allow you to design your diet while staying true to your diet.

Cooking quick, easy, and tasty meals with Cuisinart Multi-Cooker. Whether you're whipping up a fast breakfast so you can get the kids out the door, a healthy lunch so you can skip takeout, or a delicious dinner so you and your family can spend time together around the table, this comprehensive cookbook has you covered.

Chapter 1: Breakfast & Brunch

Cinnamon Roll Casserole

Preparation Time: 10 minutes

Cooking Time: 3 hours

Serve: 10

Ingredients:

- 4 eggs, lightly beaten
- 12 oz cinnamon roll tubes, refrigerated & cut into quarters
- 1 tsp ground cinnamon
- 1 1/2 tsp vanilla
- 3 tbsp maple syrup
- 1/2 cup heavy whipping cream

Directions:

1. Add half of the cinnamon roll pieces in the cooking pot.
2. In a bowl, whisk together eggs, cinnamon, vanilla, maple syrup, and heavy cream.
3. Pour egg mixture over cinnamon rolls then spread remaining rolls over the top.
4. Cover pot aura with lid.
5. Select slow cook mode and cook on LOW for 3 hours.
6. Serve and enjoy.

Nutritional Value (Amount per Serving):

- Calories 176
- Fat 7.8 g
- Carbohydrates 22.4 g
- Sugar 11.5 g
- Protein 3.9 g
- Cholesterol 74 mg

Easy Breakfast Apples

Preparation Time: 10 minutes

Cooking Time: 3 hours

Serve: 10

Ingredients:

- 9 cups apple, diced
- 2 tsp ground cinnamon
- 1 1/2 cups water
- 2 tbsp fresh lemon juice
- 1/2 tsp nutmeg

Directions:

1. Add all ingredients into the cooking pot and stir well.
2. Cover pot aura with lid.
3. Select slow cook mode and cook on HIGH for 3 hours.
4. Stir and serve.

Nutritional Value (Amount per Serving):

- Calories 107
- Fat 0.4 g
- Carbohydrates 28.2 g
- Sugar 21 g
- Protein 0.6 g
- Cholesterol 0 mg

Perfect Cranberry Eggnog Oatmeal

Preparation Time: 10 minutes

Cooking Time: 4 hours

Serve: 6

Ingredients:

- 1 cup cranberries
- 4 cups of water
- 4 cups eggnog
- 2 cups steel-cut oats

Directions:

1. Add all ingredients into the cooking pot and stir well.
2. Cover pot aura with lid.
3. Select slow cook mode and cook on LOW for 4 hours.
4. Stir well and serve.

Nutritional Value (Amount per Serving):

- Calories 342
- Fat 14.5 g
- Carbohydrates 43.1 g
- Sugar 15.2 g
- Protein 10 g
- Cholesterol 100 mg

Veggie Omelet

Preparation Time: 10 minutes

Cooking Time: 1 hour 30 minutes

Serve: 4

Ingredients:

- 6 eggs
- 4 egg whites
- 1/2 cup onion, sliced
- 1 cup spinach
- 1 mushroom, sliced
- 1/2 cup milk
- 1 tsp parsley, dried
- 1 tsp garlic powder
- 1 bell pepper, diced
- Pepper
- Salt

Directions:

1. In a large bowl, whisk together egg whites, eggs, parsley, garlic powder, almond milk, pepper, and salt.
2. Stir in mushroom, bell peppers, spinach, and onion.
3. Pour egg mixture in the cooking pot.
4. Cover pot aura with lid.
5. Select slow cook mode and cook on HIGH for 1 1/2 hours.
6. Slices and serve.

Nutritional Value (Amount per Serving):

- Calories 147
- Fat 7.4 g
- Carbohydrates 6.8 g
- Sugar 4.5 g
- Protein 13.8 g
- Cholesterol 248 mg

Cheese Herb Frittata

Preparation Time: 10 minutes

Cooking Time: 3 hours

Serve: 6

Ingredients:

- 8 eggs
- 1 tsp oregano, dried
- 3/4 cup goat cheese, crumbled
- 1/2 cup onion, sliced
- 1 1/2 cups red peppers, roasted and chopped
- 4 cups baby arugula
- 1/3 cup milk
- Pepper
- Salt

Directions:

1. In a bowl, whisk together eggs, oregano, and milk. Season with pepper and salt.
2. Arrange red peppers, onion, arugula, and cheese into the cooking pot.
3. Pour egg mixture over the vegetables.
4. Cover pot aura with lid.
5. Select slow cook mode and cook on LOW for 3 hours.
6. Serve and enjoy.

Nutritional Value (Amount per Serving):

- Calories 246
- Fat 16.9 g
- Carbohydrates 6.6 g
- Sugar 4.4 g
- Protein 18 g
- Cholesterol 250 mg

Mixed Berry Oatmeal

Preparation Time: 5 minutes

Cooking Time: 20 minutes

Serve: 4

Ingredients:

- 1 egg
- 2 cups old fashioned oats
- 1 cup blueberries
- 1/2 cup blackberries
- 1/2 cup strawberries, sliced
- 1/4 cup maple syrup
- 1 1/2 cups milk
- 1 1/2 tsp baking powder
- 1/2 tsp salt

Directions:

1. In a bowl, mix together oats, salt, and baking powder.
2. Add vanilla, egg, maple syrup, and milk and stir well. Add berries and stir well.
3. Pour mixture into the cooking pot.
4. Cover pot aura with lid.
5. Select bake mode then set the temperature to 375 F and timer for 20 minutes.
6. Serve and enjoy.

Nutritional Value (Amount per Serving):

- Calories 461
- Fat 8.4 g
- Carbohydrates 80.7 g
- Sugar 23.4 g
- Protein 15 g
- Cholesterol 48 mg

Cheesy Spinach Frittata

Preparation Time: 10 minutes

Cooking Time: 1 hour 30 minutes

Serve: 6

Ingredients:

- 3 eggs
- 3 egg whites
- 1 cup mozzarella cheese, shredded
- 1 garlic clove, minced
- 1/2 cup onion, diced
- 1 tomato, diced
- 1 cup spinach, chopped
- 2 tbsp milk
- 1 tbsp olive oil
- 1/4 tsp pepper
- Salt

Directions:

1. Add oil and onion into the cooking pot and set pot aura on saute mode and saute onion until softened.
2. In a bowl, whisk 3/4 cup mozzarella cheese, and remaining ingredients and pour in the cooking pot.
3. Top with remaining cheese.
4. Cover pot aura with lid.
5. Select slow cook mode and cook on LOW for 1 1/2 hour.
6. Serve and enjoy.

Nutritional Value (Amount per Serving):

- Calories 84
- Fat 5.5 g
- Carbohydrates 2.4 g
- Sugar 1.2 g
- Protein 6.5 g
- Cholesterol 85 mg

Healthy Veggie Frittata

Preparation Time: 10 minutes

Cooking Time: 3 hours

Serve: 4

Ingredients:

- 10 eggs
- 2 tbsp pesto
- 1 cup broccoli, chopped
- 1 cup zucchini, shredded
- 1/4 tsp red pepper flakes
- 1 tsp dried oregano
- 1 tsp garlic powder
- 1/2 cup feta cheese
- 2 tbsp fresh basil, chopped
- 2 cups kale, chopped
- 1/2 cup fennel, chopped
- 1 cup red pepper, chopped
- 1/4 cup milk
- 1/2 tsp black pepper
- 1/2 tsp salt

Directions:

1. In a large bowl, whisk eggs, feta cheese, milk, and spices.
2. Pour egg mixture in the cooking pot.
3. Add chopped vegetables and stir well.
4. Sprinkle fresh herbs on top. Top with pesto.
5. Cover pot aura with lid.
6. Select slow cook mode and cook on LOW for 3 hours.
7. Serve and enjoy.

Nutritional Value (Amount per Serving):

- Calories 295
- Fat 18.8 g
- Carbohydrates 12.9 g
- Sugar 5.4 g
- Protein 20.4 g
- Cholesterol 429 mg

Peanut Butter Banana Oatmeal

Preparation Time: 10 minutes

Cooking Time: 7 hours

Serve: 6

Ingredients:

- 2 ripe bananas, mashed
- 1 cup steel-cut oatmeal
- 2 tbsp flax seed
- 1 tsp vanilla
- 1 tsp cinnamon
- 3 tbsp brown sugar
- 3 cups of milk
- 1/4 cup peanut butter

Directions:

1. In a medium bowl, whisk together peanut butter and mashed bananas until well combined.
2. Add flaxseed, vanilla, cinnamon, brown sugar, and milk. Stir in oatmeal.
3. Pour oatmeal mixture into the cooking pot.
4. Cover pot aura with lid.
5. Select slow cook mode and cook on LOW for 7 hours.
6. Stir well and serve.

Nutritional Value (Amount per Serving):

- Calories 217
- Fat 9.3 g
- Carbohydrates 27.1 g
- Sugar 15.8 g
- Protein 8.4 g
- Cholesterol 10 mg

Almond Butter Oatmeal

Preparation Time: 5 minutes

Cooking Time: 35 minutes

Serve: 2

Ingredients:

- 2 cups old fashioned oats
- 1/2 cup almond butter
- 1/4 cup maple syrup
- 1 3/4 cup milk
- 2 tsp vanilla
- 1/4 tsp salt

Directions:

1. In a bowl, whisk together milk, vanilla, maple syrup, almond butter, and salt. Add oats and stir well.
2. Pour mixture into the cooking pot.
3. Cover pot aura with lid.
4. Select bake mode then set the temperature to 375 F and timer for 35 minutes.
5. Serve and enjoy.

Nutritional Value (Amount per Serving):

- Calories 870
- Fat 17 g
- Carbohydrates 145.6 g
- Sugar 38 g
- Protein 27.9 g
- Cholesterol 18 mg

Chapter 2: Vegetarian & Vegan

Cheesy Squash

Preparation Time: 10 minutes

Cooking Time: 1 hour 30 minutes

Serve: 8

Ingredients:

- 4 medium yellow squash, cut into half-moon shapes
- 6 oz Velveeta cheese, cubed
- 4 tbsp butter, cubed
- 1 small onion, sliced
- Pepper
- salt

Directions:

1. Add squash and onion into the cooking pot. Season with pepper and salt.
2. Add cheese and butter on top of the squash and onion mixture.
3. Cover pot aura with lid.
4. Select slow cook mode and cook on LOW for 1 1/2 hours.
5. Serve and enjoy.

Nutritional Value (Amount per Serving):

- Calories 131
- Fat 10.5 g
- Carbohydrates 6.4 g
- Sugar 3.6 g
- Protein 5.2 g
- Cholesterol 30 mg

Lemon Butter Carrots

Preparation Time: 10 minutes

Cooking Time: 3 hours

Serve: 4

Ingredients:

- 2 lbs carrots, cut into matchsticks
- 1 tbsp lemon zest
- 1/4 cup fresh lemon juice
- 1 tbsp fresh thyme, chopped
- 1/4 cup butter
- 1 onion, diced
- Pepper
- Salt

Directions:

1. Add all ingredients into the cooking pot and stir well.
2. Cover pot aura with lid.
3. Select slow cook mode and cook on HIGH for 3 hours.
4. Stir well and serve.

Nutritional Value (Amount per Serving):

- Calories 212
- Fat 11.7 g
- Carbohydrates 26 g
- Sugar 12.7 g
- Protein 2.5 g
- Cholesterol 31 mg

Slow Cook Potatoes

Preparation Time: 10 minutes

Cooking Time: 8 hours

Serve: 6

Ingredients:

- 3 lbs potatoes, halved
- 1/8 tsp cayenne pepper
- 1/4 tsp garlic powder
- 1 1/4 tsp dried oregano
- 1 1/4 tsp paprika
- 1/4 cup butter, melted
- 1 onion, halved
- Pepper
- Salt

Directions:

1. Add all ingredients into the cooking pot and stir well.
2. Cover pot aura with lid.
3. Select slow cook mode and cook on LOW for 8 hours.
4. Stir well and serve.

Nutritional Value (Amount per Serving):

- Calories 234
- Fat 8 g
- Carbohydrates 37.9 g
- Sugar 3.5 g
- Protein 4.2 g
- Cholesterol 20 mg

Garlic Cauliflower Grits

Preparation Time: 10 minutes

Cooking Time: 2 hours

Serve: 8

Ingredients:

- 6 cups cauliflower rice
- 1/2 cup vegetable stock
- 1/4 tsp onion powder
- 1/4 tsp garlic powder
- 1 cup cream cheese
- 1/2 tsp pepper
- 1 tsp salt

Directions:

1. Add all ingredients into the cooking pot and stir well.
2. Cover pot aura with lid.
3. Select slow cook mode and cook on LOW for 2 hours.
4. Stir well and serve.

Nutritional Value (Amount per Serving):

- Calories 145
- Fat 11.5 g
- Carbohydrates 6.1 g
- Sugar 3.2 g
- Protein 5.2 g
- Cholesterol 32 mg

Coconut Lentil Vegetable Curry

Preparation Time: 10 minutes

Cooking Time: 8 hours

Serve: 10

Ingredients:

- 2 cups brown lentils
- 15 oz can tomato sauce
- 15 oz can tomato, diced
- 2 carrots, peel and diced
- 1 sweet potato, peel and diced
- 2 garlic cloves, minced
- 1 onion, diced
- 14 oz can coconut milk
- 3 cups vegetable broth
- 1/4 tsp ground cloves
- 3 tbsp curry powder

Directions:

1. Add all ingredients except milk into the cooking pot and stir well.
2. Cover pot aura with lid.
3. Select slow cook mode and cook on LOW for 8 hours.
4. Stir in coconut milk and serve.

Nutritional Value (Amount per Serving):

- Calories 106
- Fat 3.2 g
- Carbohydrates 15.3 g
- Sugar 6.8 g
- Protein 5.1 g
- Cholesterol 0 mg

Easy Vegan Gumbo

Preparation Time: 10 minutes

Cooking Time: 8 hours

Serve: 6

Ingredients:

- 2 large carrots, peeled & chopped
- 2 celery stalks, chopped
- 1 green bell pepper, chopped
- 1 small onion, chopped
- 1/4 cup fresh parsley, chopped
- 2 tbsp tomato paste
- 1/2 tsp dried thyme
- 2 tbsp cajun seasoning
- 2 tbsp soy sauce
- 1 1/2 cups mushrooms, cut into quarters
- 1 1/2 cups asparagus, chopped
- 30 oz can kidney beans, rinsed & drained
- 30 oz can tomato, diced
- 3 cups vegetable broth
- 1 tbsp garlic, minced
- 1/4 tsp kosher salt

Directions:

1. Add all ingredients except parsley into the cooking pot and stir well.
2. Cover pot aura with lid.
3. Select slow cook mode and cook on LOW for 8 hours.
4. Garnish with parsley and serve.

Nutritional Value (Amount per Serving):

- Calories 211
- Fat 1.4 g
- Carbohydrates 38.8 g
- Sugar 12.3 g
- Protein 13.8 g
- Cholesterol 0 mg

Delicious Thai Pineapple Curry

Preparation Time: 10 minutes

Cooking Time: 6 hours

Serve: 4

Ingredients:

- 1 fresh pineapple, cut into 1-inch pieces
- 3 cups garbanzo beans, soaked overnight in water & drained
- 2 onions, cut into 1-inch pieces
- 2 green bell pepper, cut into 1-inch pieces
- 1 lb sweet potatoes, peel & cut into 1-inch pieces
- 1 1/2 tsp granulated garlic
- 1 tsp crushed red pepper
- 3 tbsp curry powder
- 14.5 oz can coconut milk
- 1 1/2 tsp salt

Directions:

1. Add coconut milk, curry powder, crushed red pepper, garlic, and salt into the cooking pot and stir well.
2. Add remaining ingredients and stir well.
3. Cover pot aura with lid.
4. Select slow cook mode and cook on LOW for 6 hours.
5. Stir well and serve.

Nutritional Value (Amount per Serving):

- Calories 613
- Fat 24.6 g
- Carbohydrates 84.8 g
- Sugar 10.4 g
- Protein 16.6 g
- Cholesterol 0 mg

Parmesan Zucchini

Preparation Time: 10 minutes

Cooking Time: 3 hours

Serve: 3

Ingredients:

- 2 zucchini, cut into half-moons
- 1/4 cup parmesan cheese, grated
- 1/2 tsp Italian seasoning
- 1 tbsp olive oil
- 1 tbsp butter
- 1 tbsp garlic, minced
- 1 onion, sliced
- 2 tomatoes, diced
- 1/2 tsp pepper
- 1/4 tsp salt

Directions:

1. Add all ingredients except cheese into the cooking pot and stir well.
2. Cover pot aura with lid.
3. Select slow cook mode and cook on LOW for 3 hours.
4. Top with cheese and serve.

Nutritional Value (Amount per Serving):

- Calories 194
- Fat 13.3 g
- Carbohydrates 12.9 g
- Sugar 6.1 g
- Protein 9.2 g
- Cholesterol 25 mg

Beans & Potatoes

Preparation Time: 10 minutes

Cooking Time: 4 hours

Serve: 6

Ingredients:

- 1 lb green beans, trimmed and cut
- 1 lb potatoes, sliced in half
- 2 shallots, sliced
- 1 tbsp red wine vinegar
- 4 tbsp butter
- 2 cups vegetable broth
- 2 cups of water
- Pepper
- Salt

Directions:

1. Add all ingredients into the cooking pot and stir well.
2. Cover pot aura with lid.
3. Select slow cook mode and cook on HIGH for 4 hours.
4. Serve and enjoy.

Nutritional Value (Amount per Serving):

- Calories 159
- Fat 8.3 g
- Carbohydrates 18.2 g
- Sugar 2.2 g
- Protein 4.4 g
- Cholesterol 20 mg

Parmesan Squash Casserole

Preparation Time: 10 minutes

Cooking Time: 6 hours

Serve: 6

Ingredients:

- 2 cups yellow squash, quartered and sliced
- 2 cups zucchini, quartered and sliced
- 1 tsp garlic powder
- 1 tsp Italian seasoning
- 1/4 cup parmesan cheese, grated
- 1/4 cup butter, cut into pieces
- 1/4 tsp pepper
- 1/2 tsp sea salt

Directions:

1. Add sliced yellow squash and zucchini into the cooking pot.
2. Sprinkle with garlic powder, Italian seasoning, pepper, and salt.
3. Top with cheese and butter.
4. Cover pot aura with lid.
5. Select slow cook mode and cook on LOW for 6 hours.
6. Serve and enjoy.

Nutritional Value (Amount per Serving):

- Calories 115
- Fat 10.1 g
- Carbohydrates 3.4 g
- Sugar 1.5 g
- Protein 4.2 g
- Cholesterol 28 mg

Chapter 3: Beans & Grains

BBQ Beans

Preparation Time: 10 minutes

Cooking Time: 6 hours

Serve: 16

Ingredients:

- 15 oz can kidney beans, drained & rinsed
- 30 oz can great northern beans, drained & rinsed
- 30 oz can black beans, drained & rinsed
- 2 lbs kielbasa, cut into bite-size pieces
- 1/2 lb bacon, cooked & chopped
- 14 oz chicken broth
- 1/4 cup molasses
- 1/2 cup maple syrup
- 1 tbsp apple cider vinegar
- 1 tsp chili powder
- 1 tbsp mustard
- 1 tbsp Worcestershire sauce
- 3/4 cup ketchup
- 1/2 cup BBQ sauce
- 1 onion, diced

Directions:

1. Add all ingredients except kielbasa into the cooking pot and stir well.
2. Top with kielbasa and stir gently.
3. Cover pot aura with lid.
4. Select slow cook mode and cook on LOW for 6 hours.
5. Stir and serve.

Nutritional Value (Amount per Serving):

- Calories 412
- Fat 16.9 g
- Carbohydrates 44.5 g
- Sugar 14.8 g
- Protein 21.8 g
- Cholesterol 55 mg

Jerk Seasoned Black Beans

Preparation Time: 10 minutes

Cooking Time: 5 hours

Serve: 6

Ingredients:

- 1 lb black beans, soak in water for overnight & drain
- 14 oz tomatoes, chopped
- 1 bay leaf
- 1 tsp jerk seasoning
- 1 red pepper, chopped
- 1 chili pepper, chopped
- 2 garlic cloves, chopped
- 5 cups vegetable broth
- 2 tbsp fresh lime juice
- 1 large onion, chopped
- 2 tbsp olive oil

Directions:

1. Add oil, onion, garlic, peppers, and seasoning into the cooking pot and set pot aura on saute mode and saute until onion is softened.
2. Add remaining ingredients into the cooking pot and stir well.
3. Cover pot aura with lid.
4. Select slow cook mode and cook on HIGH for 5 hours.
5. Stir well and serve.

Nutritional Value (Amount per Serving):

- Calories 364
- Fat 7.1 g
- Carbohydrates 56 g
- Sugar 6.3 g
- Protein 21.6 g
- Cholesterol 0 mg

Parmesan Risotto

Preparation Time: 10 minutes
Cooking Time: 2 hours
Serve: 5

Ingredients:

- 3/4 cup parmesan cheese, shredded
- 1 1/4 cups Arborio rice
- 4 tbsp white wine
- 4 tbsp olive oil
- 1 tbsp garlic powder
- 4 cups vegetable broth
- 1/2 tsp pepper
- 1/2 tsp salt

Directions:

1. Add all ingredients except cheese into the cooking pot and stir well.
2. Cover pot aura with lid.
3. Select slow cook mode and cook on HIGH for 2 hours.
4. Add cheese and stir until cheese is melted & serve.

Nutritional Value (Amount per Serving):

- Calories 427
- Fat 20.1 g
- Carbohydrates 41.5 g
- Sugar 1.1 g
- Protein 18.7 g
- Cholesterol 25 mg

Baked Beans

Preparation Time: 10 minutes

Cooking Time: 8 hours

Serve: 10

Ingredients:

- 3 cups dried navy beans, soaked in water for overnight & drained
- 4 cups chicken broth
- 1/4 cup molasses
- 3/4 cup brown sugar
- 15 oz can tomato sauce
- 1/4 tsp cayenne pepper
- 1 tsp black pepper
- 1 tbsp ground mustard
- 1 bell pepper, diced
- 1 onion, diced
- 1 lb bacon, cut into 1-inch pieces
- 1 tbsp kosher salt

Directions:

1. Add bacon, bell pepper, and onion into the cooking pot and set pot aura on saute mode.
2. Saute until onion softens.
3. Add remaining ingredients into the cooking pot and stir well.
4. Cover pot aura with lid.
5. Select slow cook mode and cook on LOW for 8 hours.
6. Stir and serve.

Nutritional Value (Amount per Serving):

- Calories 561
- Fat 20.9 g
- Carbohydrates 60.5 g
- Sugar 20.8 g
- Protein 33.8 g
- Cholesterol 50 mg

Jalapeno Pinto Beans

Preparation Time: 10 minutes

Cooking Time: 8 hours

Serve: 6

Ingredients:

- 1 lb pinto beans, soak in water for overnight & drain
- 14 oz beef broth
- 32 oz vegetable broth
- 6 bacon sliced, cooked & chopped
- 2 jalapeno peppers, seeded & chopped
- 15 oz can tomato, diced & drained
- 1 tsp garlic powder
- 1 tsp cumin
- 1 tsp black pepper
- 1 tbsp garlic, minced
- 1 onion, sliced

Directions:

1. Add all ingredients into the cooking pot and stir well.
2. Cover pot aura with lid.
3. Select slow cook mode and cook on HIGH for 8 hours.
4. Stir and serve.

Nutritional Value (Amount per Serving):

- Calories 441
- Fat 5.4 g
- Carbohydrates 55 g
- Sugar 5.7 g
- Protein 30.8 g
- Cholesterol 50 mg

BBQ Lima Beans

Preparation Time: 10 minutes

Cooking Time: 6 hours

Serve: 20

Ingredients:

- 1 1/2 lbs dried lima beans, soak in water for overnight & drain
- 1/4 lb bacon, diced
- 1/2 cup corn syrup
- 10 drops Tabasco sauce
- 1 1/2 cup ketchup
- 1/2 cup brown sugar
- 2 1/4 cups onions, chopped
- 6 cups of water
- 1 tsp salt

Directions:

1. Add all ingredients into the cooking pot and stir well.
2. Cover pot aura with lid.
3. Select slow cook mode and cook on HIGH for 6 hours.
4. Stir and serve.

Nutritional Value (Amount per Serving):

- Calories 129
- Fat 2.8 g
- Carbohydrates 22.1 g
- Sugar 10.7 g
- Protein 4.9 g
- Cholesterol 6 mg

Spinach Barley Risotto

Preparation Time: 10 minutes

Cooking Time: 6 hours

Serve: 4

Ingredients:

- 1 cup pearl barley
- 1/2 cup halloumi, cut into small pieces
- 2 1/2 cups fresh spinach, chopped
- 2 1/2 cups vegetable stock
- 2 garlic cloves, chopped
- 1 onion, chopped

Directions:

1. Add barley, stock, garlic, and onion into the cooking pot and stir well.
2. Cover pot aura with lid.
3. Select slow cook mode and cook on LOW for 6 hours.
4. Add spinach and stir until spinach is wilted.
5. Top with halloumi and serve.

Nutritional Value (Amount per Serving):

- Calories 237
- Fat 3.9 g
- Carbohydrates 43.6 g
- Sugar 2.1 g
- Protein 8.8 g
- Cholesterol 8 mg

Delicious Refried Beans

Preparation Time: 10 minutes

Cooking Time: 8 hours

Serve: 6

Ingredients:

- 1 lb dry pinto beans, soak in water for overnight & drained
- 1 tsp cumin
- 2 tsp pepper
- 2 tbsp garlic, minced
- 1 jalapeno pepper, cut the top and quartered
- 1 onion, quartered
- 4 cups vegetable stock
- 5 cups of water
- 3 tsp salt

Directions:

1. Add all ingredients into the cooking pot and stir well.
2. Cover pot aura with lid.
3. Select slow cook mode and cook on HIGH for 8 hours.
4. Drain water from beans and mash the beans using an immersion blender until get desired consistency.
5. Stir well and serve.

Nutritional Value (Amount per Serving):

- Calories 282
- Fat 1.1 g
- Carbohydrates 51.3 g
- Sugar 3 g
- Protein 17 g
- Cholesterol 0 mg

Bacon Bean Chowder

Preparation Time: 10 minutes

Cooking Time: 8 hours

Serve: 6

Ingredients:

- 1 1/2 cup dried navy beans, soak in water for overnight & drain
- 1 celery stalk, sliced
- 2 medium carrots, sliced
- 8 bacon slices, cooked and crumbled
- 1/8 tsp pepper
- 1 cup milk
- 46 oz can chicken broth
- 1 tsp Italian seasoning
- 1 medium onion, chopped

Directions:

1. Add all ingredients except milk into the cooking pot and stir well.
2. Cover pot aura with lid.
3. Select slow cook mode and cook on LOW for 8 hours.
4. Transfer 2 cups of beans into the blender and blend until smooth.
5. Return blended beans into the cooking pot and stir well.
6. Add milk and stir well. Cover and cook on high for 10 minutes more.
7. Stir well and serve.

Nutritional Value (Amount per Serving):

- Calories 751
- Fat 30.1 g
- Carbohydrates 39.6 g
- Sugar 5.7 g
- Protein 77.7 g
- Cholesterol 140 mg

Old Fashioned Lima Beans

Preparation Time: 10 minutes

Cooking Time: 4 hours

Serve: 10

Ingredients:

- 1 lb dried lima beans, soak in water for overnight & drained
- 4 cups chicken broth
- 1 tsp chili powder
- 1 tsp garlic, minced
- 2 onions, chopped
- 3 cups meaty ham hocks
- Pepper
- Salt

Directions:

1. Add all ingredients into the cooking pot and stir well.
2. Cover pot aura with lid.
3. Select slow cook mode and cook on LOW for 4 hours.
4. Stir well and serve.

Nutritional Value (Amount per Serving):

- Calories 188
- Fat 8.8 g
- Carbohydrates 11.8 g
- Sugar 1.9 g
- Protein 14.6 g
- Cholesterol 36 mg

Chapter 4: Soup & Stews

Flavorful White Chicken Chili

Preparation Time: 10 minutes

Cooking Time: 8 hours

Serve: 8

Ingredients:

- 4 chicken breasts, skinless & boneless
- 1 tsp dried oregano
- 1 tsp ground cumin
- 1 tbsp chili powder
- 1 jalapeno pepper, minced
- 8 oz can green chilies, chopped
- 30 oz can great northern beans, drained & rinsed
- 2 garlic cloves, minced
- 1 small onion, chopped
- 6 cups chicken broth

Directions:

1. Add all ingredients into the cooking pot and stir well.
2. Cover pot aura with lid.
3. Select slow cook mode and cook on LOW for 8 hours.
4. Remove chicken from cooking pot and shred using a fork.
5. Return shredded chicken to the cooking pot and stir well.
6. Serve and enjoy.

Nutritional Value (Amount per Serving):

- Calories 304
- Fat 7.2 g
- Carbohydrates 26.3 g
- Sugar 1.1 g
- Protein 33.2 g
- Cholesterol 65 mg

Curried Coconut Pumpkin Soup

Preparation Time: 10 minutes

Cooking Time: 5 hours

Serve: 6

Ingredients:

- 30 oz pumpkin puree
- 4 cups vegetable broth
- 14 oz coconut milk
- 2 tbsp red curry paste

Directions:

1. Add all ingredients into the cooking pot and stir well.
2. Cover pot aura with lid.
3. Select slow cook mode and cook on LOW for 5 hours.
4. Stir well and serve.

Nutritional Value (Amount per Serving):

- Calories 246
- Fat 18.6 g
- Carbohydrates 16.7 g
- Sugar 7.4 g
- Protein 6.3 g
- Cholesterol 0 mg

Creamy Asparagus Soup

Preparation Time: 10 minutes

Cooking Time: 8 hours

Serve: 4

Ingredients:

- 1 lb asparagus, ends trimmed and chopped
- 2 garlic cloves, minced
- 1 large onion, diced
- 1 tsp lemon juice
- 1/2 cup coconut yogurt
- 3 cups vegetable stock
- Pepper
- Salt

Directions:

1. Add all ingredients except coconut yogurt and lemon juice into the cooking pot and stir well.
2. Cover pot aura with lid.
3. Select slow cook mode and cook on LOW for 8 hours.
4. Puree the soup until smooth. Return soup into the cooking pot.
5. Stir in coconut yogurt and lemon juice.
6. Stir well and serve.

Nutritional Value (Amount per Serving):

- Calories 69
- Fat 1.1 g
- Carbohydrates 12.2 g
- Sugar 7.1 g
- Protein 4.4 g
- Cholesterol 0 mg

Healthy & Creamy Asparagus Soup

Preparation Time: 10 minutes

Cooking Time: 8 hours

Serve: 8

Ingredients:

- 2 lbs asparagus, wash and trim
- 1 cup onion, chopped
- 1/2 cup coconut milk
- 5 cups of water
- Pepper
- Salt

Directions:

1. Add all ingredients except coconut milk into the cooking pot and stir well.
2. Cover pot aura with lid.
3. Select slow cook mode and cook on LOW for 8 hours.
4. Puree the soup until smooth, return soup into the cooking pot.
5. Stir in coconut milk and serve.

Nutritional Value (Amount per Serving):

- Calories 63
- Fat 3.7 g
- Carbohydrates 6.6 g
- Sugar 3.2 g
- Protein 3 g
- Cholesterol 0 mg

Easy Cauliflower Leek Soup

Preparation Time: 10 minutes

Cooking Time: 8 hours

Serve: 2

Ingredients:

- 4 1/2 cups cauliflower florets
- 1 tbsp olive oil
- 2 cups leeks
- 2 cups vegetable stock
- 1 tsp salt

Directions:

1. Add all ingredients into the cooking pot and stir well.
2. Cover pot aura with lid.
3. Select slow cook mode and cook on LOW for 8 hours.
4. Puree the soup until smooth and serve.

Nutritional Value (Amount per Serving):

- Calories 177
- Fat 7.6 g
- Carbohydrates 25.4 g
- Sugar 9.6 g
- Protein 6.2 g
- Cholesterol 0 mg

Flavors Stuffed Cabbage Soup

Preparation Time: 10 minutes

Cooking Time: 4 hours

Serve: 8

Ingredients:

- 1/2 cabbage head, cut into 1-inch pieces
- 1 tsp basil
- 1 tsp oregano
- 1 tbsp garlic salt
- 1 lb ground beef
- 19 oz tomato soup
- 23 oz jar spaghetti sauce
- 1 tbsp Worcestershire sauce
- 42 oz beef broth
- 2/3 cup rice, uncooked

Directions:

1. Add ground beef and onion into the cooking pot and set pot aura on saute mode.
2. Saute meat until brown.
3. Add remaining ingredients into the cooking pot and stir well.
4. Cover pot aura with lid.
5. Select slow cook mode and cook on HIGH for 4 hours.
6. Stir well and serve.

Nutritional Value (Amount per Serving):

- Calories 293
- Fat 6.8 g
- Carbohydrates 33.9 g
- Sugar 14.9 g
- Protein 24.4 g
- Cholesterol 51 mg

Italian Tomato Soup

Preparation Time: 10 minutes

Cooking Time: 6 hours

Serve: 4

Ingredients:

- 28 oz tomatoes, chopped
- 2 garlic cloves, chopped
- 1/2 onion, chopped
- 1 tsp Italian seasoning
- 1/4 cup olive oil
- 1/2 cup heavy cream
- 1/2 cup ricotta cheese
- 1/4 cup chicken stock

Directions:

1. Add all ingredients except heavy cream and cheese into the cooking pot and stir well.
2. Cover pot aura with lid.
3. Select slow cook mode and cook on LOW for 6 hours.
4. Puree the soup using a blender until smooth. Return soup into the cooking pot.
5. Stir in cheese and heavy cream.
6. Stir well and serve.

Nutritional Value (Amount per Serving):

- Calories 250
- Fat 21.4 g
- Carbohydrates 11.7 g
- Sugar 6.1 g
- Protein 5.9 g
- Cholesterol 31 mg

Chickpea Stew

Preparation Time: 10 minutes

Cooking Time: 4 hours

Serve: 4

Ingredients:

- 16 oz can chickpeas, drained
- 1 onion, chopped
- 1/2 tsp dried rosemary, crushed
- 2 lbs stew beef, cut into cubes
- 1/2 cup chicken stock
- 10 oz can tomatoes, diced
- 1 carrot, peeled and sliced
- 1 tbsp olive oil
- Pepper
- Salt

Directions:

1. Add oil and meat into the cooking pot and set pot aura on sauté mode and sauté meat until brown.
2. Add remaining ingredients into the cooking pot and stir well.
3. Cover pot aura with lid.
4. Select slow cook mode and cook on LOW for 4 hours.
5. Stir well and serve.

Nutritional Value (Amount per Serving):

- Calories 530
- Fat 18.5 g
- Carbohydrates 33.5 g
- Sugar 4.4 g
- Protein 56.7 g
- Cholesterol 0 mg

Hearty Beef Stew

Preparation Time: 10 minutes

Cooking Time: 8 hours

Serve: 6

Ingredients:

- 1 lb beef stew cubes
- 10 oz frozen green peas
- 8 oz can tomato sauce
- 20 oz can cream of mushroom soup
- 1 oz dry onion soup mix
- 1 bay leaf
- 4 potatoes, cubed
- 4 carrots, sliced
- Pepper
- Salt

Directions:

1. Add all ingredients into the cooking pot and stir well.
2. Cover pot aura with lid.
3. Select slow cook mode and cook on LOW for 8 hours.
4. Stir well and serve.

Nutritional Value (Amount per Serving):

- Calories 297
- Fat 6.1 g
- Carbohydrates 51.1 g
- Sugar 10.9 g
- Protein 11 g
- Cholesterol 15 mg

Mushroom Beef Stew

Preparation Time: 10 minutes

Cooking Time: 8 hours

Serve: 8

Ingredients:

- 2 lbs stewing beef, cubed
- 4 oz can mushroom, sliced
- 1/2 cup water
- 1 packet dry onion soup mix
- 14 oz cream of mushroom soup
- 1/4 tsp black pepper
- 1/2 tsp salt

Directions:

1. Add all ingredients into the cooking pot and stir well.
2. Cover pot aura with lid.
3. Select slow cook mode and cook on LOW for 8 hours.
4. Stir well and serve.

Nutritional Value (Amount per Serving):

- Calories 238
- Fat 8.5 g
- Carbohydrates 2.9 g
- Sugar 0.4 g
- Protein 35.2 g
- Cholesterol 101 mg

Chapter 5: Poultry

Curried Chicken Thighs

Preparation Time: 10 minutes

Cooking Time: 4 hours

Serve: 4

Ingredients:

- 1 1/2 lbs chicken thighs
- 2 tbsp fresh ginger, minced
- 1 tsp cumin
- 1 tsp turmeric
- 1 tsp garam masala
- 1 cinnamon stick
- 2 bay leaves
- 1 medium onion, diced
- 1/4 cup fresh cilantro, chopped
- 2 tbsp tomato paste
- 14 oz can coconut milk
- 3 garlic cloves, minced
- 1 1/2 tsp salt

Directions:

1. Add all ingredients into the cooking pot and stir well.
2. Cover pot aura with lid.
3. Select slow cook mode and cook on LOW for 4 hours.
4. Shred the chicken using a fork.
5. Stir well and serve.

Nutritional Value (Amount per Serving):

- Calories 555
- Fat 34.2 g
- Carbohydrates 10.8 g
- Sugar 2.3 g
- Protein 52.5 g
- Cholesterol 151 mg

Mustard Mushroom Chicken

Preparation Time: 10 minutes

Cooking Time: 6 hours

Serve: 4

Ingredients:

- 4 chicken thighs, bone-in & skin-on
- 1 tsp garlic, minced
- 1 tsp grainy mustard
- 8 oz mushrooms, sliced
- 10.5 oz cream of mushroom soup
- Pepper
- Salt

Directions:

1. Season chicken with pepper and salt and place into the cooking pot.
2. Mix together remaining ingredients and pour over chicken.
3. Cover pot aura with lid.
4. Select slow cook mode and cook on LOW for 6 hours.
5. Serve and enjoy.

Nutritional Value (Amount per Serving):

- Calories 324
- Fat 13.3 g
- Carbohydrates 4.7 g
- Sugar 1.5 g
- Protein 44.8 g
- Cholesterol 130 mg

Tasty Chicken Fajita Pasta

Preparation Time: 10 minutes

Cooking Time: 6 hours

Serve: 6

Ingredients:

- 2 chicken breasts, skinless & boneless
- 2 cups cheddar cheese, shredded
- 16 oz penne pasta, cooked
- 2 cups chicken broth
- 10 oz can tomato, diced
- 2 tsp garlic, minced
- 1 bell peppers, diced
- 1/2 onion, diced
- 2 tbsp taco seasoning

Directions:

1. Add all ingredients except cheese and pasta into the cooking pot and stir well.
2. Cover pot aura with lid.
3. Select slow cook mode and cook on LOW for 6 hours.
4. Stir in cheese and pasta.
5. Serve and enjoy.

Nutritional Value (Amount per Serving):

- Calories 620
- Fat 25.2 g
- Carbohydrates 56.2 g
- Sugar 3.4 g
- Protein 41.3 g
- Cholesterol 157 mg

Flavors Peanut Butter Chicken

Preparation Time: 10 minutes

Cooking Time: 8 hours

Serve: 4

Ingredients:

- 3 lbs chicken breasts, bone-in & skinless
- 3 tbsp maple syrup
- 1/2 tbsp rice wine vinegar
- 1 tbsp coarse whole grain mustard
- 1 tbsp garlic, minced
- 2 tbsp chili garlic sauce
- 1/2 cup soy sauce
- 1/2 lime juice
- 1/4 cup peanut butter
- Pepper
- salt

Directions:

1. Season chicken with pepper and salt and place into the cooking pot.
2. Mix together remaining ingredients and pour over chicken in the cooking pot.
3. Cover pot aura with lid.
4. Select slow cook mode and cook on LOW for 8 hours.
5. Remove chicken from pot and shred using a fork.
6. Serve and enjoy.

Nutritional Value (Amount per Serving):

- Calories 806
- Fat 33.5 g
- Carbohydrates 17.1 g
- Sugar 11.1 g
- Protein 104.6 g
- Cholesterol 303 mg

Greek Lemon Chicken

Preparation Time: 10 minutes

Cooking Time: 6 hours

Serve: 4

Ingredients:

- 4 chicken breasts, skinless & boneless
- 3 tbsp parsley, chopped
- 1 cup chicken broth
- 1 tbsp lemon zest
- 1/4 cup lemon juice
- 2 tsp dried oregano
- 1 tbsp garlic, minced
- 1 tsp kosher salt

Directions:

1. Add all ingredients into the cooking pot and mix well.
2. Cover pot aura with lid.
3. Select slow cook mode and cook on LOW for 6 hours.
4. Serve and enjoy.

Nutritional Value (Amount per Serving):

- Calories 296
- Fat 11.3 g
- Carbohydrates 1.7 g
- Sugar 0.6 g
- Protein 43.8 g
- Cholesterol 130 mg

Ginger Garlic Broccoli Chicken

Preparation Time: 10 minutes

Cooking Time: 8 hours

Serve: 8

Ingredients:

- 4 chicken breast, skinless, boneless, and halves
- 1 garlic clove, chopped
- 1/4 cup white miso
- 2 cups chicken stock
- 1 lb broccoli florets
- 1 tbsp ginger, sliced

Directions:

1. Add all ingredients into the cooking pot and stir well.
2. Cover pot aura with lid.
3. Select slow cook mode and cook on LOW for 8 hours.
4. Stir well and serve.

Nutritional Value (Amount per Serving):

- Calories 99
- Fat 2.1 g
- Carbohydrates 6.8 g
- Sugar 1.7 g
- Protein 13.4 g
- Cholesterol 32 mg

Pesto Chicken

Preparation Time: 10 minutes

Cooking Time: 7 hours

Serve: 2

Ingredients:

- 2 chicken breasts, skinless and boneless
- 2 cups cherry tomatoes, halved
- 2 tbsp basil pesto
- 2 cups zucchini, chopped
- 2 cups green beans, chopped

Directions:

1. Add all ingredients into the cooking pot and stir well.
2. Cover pot aura with lid.
3. Select slow cook mode and cook on LOW for 7 hours.
4. Stir well and serve.

Nutritional Value (Amount per Serving):

- Calories 26
- Fat 0.8 g
- Carbohydrates 1.3 g
- Sugar 0.6 g
- Protein 3.4 g
- Cholesterol 9 mg

Buffalo Chicken Drumsticks

Preparation Time: 10 minutes

Cooking Time: 4 hours

Serve: 6

Ingredients:

- 8 chicken drumsticks, skin removed
- 3 tbsp dried parsley
- 1/2 cup dry wine
- 1/2 cup hot sauce
- 3 garlic cloves, minced
- 1/4 cup olive oil

Directions:

1. Add all ingredients into the large zip-lock bag and place it in the fridge for 3 hours.
2. Pour marinated chicken into the cooking pot.
3. Cover pot aura with lid.
4. Select slow cook mode and cook on LOW for 4 hours.
5. Stir well and serve.

Nutritional Value (Amount per Serving):

- Calories 197
- Fat 12 g
- Carbohydrates 1.5 g
- Sugar 0.4 g
- Protein 17.1 g
- Cholesterol 54 mg

Thai Chicken Wings

Preparation Time: 10 minutes

Cooking Time: 6 hours

Serve: 6

Ingredients:

- 3 lbs chicken wings
- 2 oz Thai basil, minced
- 8 oz green curry paste
- 1 tbsp coconut milk
- 1 tbsp fresh cilantro, minced
- 1 tbsp fresh ginger, minced

Directions:

1. Add chicken wings in the cooking pot.
2. In a bowl, whisk the coconut milk with cilantro, ginger, basil, and curry paste.
3. Pour coconut milk mixture over chicken wings.
4. Cover pot aura with lid.
5. Select slow cook mode and cook on LOW for 6 hours.
6. Serve and enjoy.

Nutritional Value (Amount per Serving):

- Calories 537
- Fat 23.8 g
- Carbohydrates 10.5 g
- Sugar 0.1 g
- Protein 66.1 g
- Cholesterol 202 mg

Tomatillo Chicken

Preparation Time: 10 minutes

Cooking Time: 6 hours

Serve: 6

Ingredients:

- 6 chicken drumsticks, bone-in, and skin removed
- 1 1/2 cups tomatillo sauce
- 1 tbsp apple cider vinegar
- 1 tsp olive oil
- 1 tsp dried oregano
- Pepper
- Salt

Directions:

1. Add all ingredients into the cooking pot and stir well.
2. Cover pot aura with lid.
3. Select slow cook mode and cook on LOW for 6 hours.
4. Stir well and serve.

Nutritional Value (Amount per Serving):

- Calories 95
- Fat 3.4 g
- Carbohydrates 2.1 g
- Sugar 1 g
- Protein 12.7 g
- Cholesterol 40 mg

Chapter 6: Beef, Pork & Lamb

Delicious Sweet Pork Roast

Preparation Time: 10 minutes

Cooking Time: 8 hours

Serve: 6

Ingredients:

- 2 lbs pork roast, boneless
- 1 cup brown sugar
- 2 cups salsa

Directions:

1. Place pork roast into the cooking pot.
- Mix together brown sugar and salsa and pour over pork roast in the cooking pot.
2. Cover pot aura with lid.
3. Select slow cook mode and cook on LOW for 8 hours.
4. Shred pork roast using the fork and serve.

Nutritional Value (Amount per Serving):

- Calories 428
- Fat 14.4 g
- Carbohydrates 29.1 g
- Sugar 26.1 g
- Protein 44.5 g
- Cholesterol 130 mg

Olive Feta Beef

Preparation Time: 10 minutes

Cooking Time: 6 hours

Serve: 6

Ingredients:

- 2 lbs beef stew meat, cut into half-inch pieces
- 1 cup olives, pitted and cut in half
- 30 oz can tomato, diced
- 1/2 cup feta cheese, crumbled
- 1/4 tsp pepper
- 12 tsp salt

Directions:

1. Add all ingredients into the cooking pot and stir well.
2. Cover pot aura with lid.
3. Select slow cook mode and cook on HIGH for 6 hours.
4. Serve and enjoy.

Nutritional Value (Amount per Serving):

- Calories 370
- Fat 14.5 g
- Carbohydrates 9.2 g
- Sugar 5.3 g
- Protein 49.1 g
- Cholesterol 146 mg

Garlic Tomatoes Chuck Roast

Preparation Time: 10 minutes

Cooking Time: 10 hours

Serve: 6

Ingredients:

- 2 lbs beef chuck roast
- 1/2 cup beef broth
- 1/4 cup sun-dried tomatoes, chopped
- 25 garlic cloves, peeled
- 1/4 cup olives, sliced
- 1 tsp dried Italian seasoning, crushed
- 2 tbsp balsamic vinegar

Directions:

1. Add the meat into the cooking pot then mix together the remaining ingredients except for couscous and pour over the meat.
2. Cover pot aura with lid.
3. Select slow cook mode and cook on LOW for 8 hours.
4. Remove meat from pot and shred using a fork.
5. Return shredded meat to the pot and stir well.

Nutritional Value (Amount per Serving):

- Calories 582
- Fat 43.1 g
- Carbohydrates 5 g
- Sugar 0.5 g
- Protein 40.8 g
- Cholesterol 156 mg

Herb Lamb Chops

Preparation Time: 10 minutes

Cooking Time: 6 hours

Serve: 4

Ingredients:

- 8 lamb chops
- 2 garlic cloves, minced
- 1 tsp dried oregano
- 1 onion, sliced
- 1/2 tsp garlic powder
- 1/2 tsp dried thyme
- 1/8 tsp black pepper
- 1/4 tsp salt

Directions:

1. Place sliced onion into the cooking pot.
2. In a small bowl, combine together oregano, garlic powder, thyme, pepper, and salt.
3. Rub oregano mixture over the lamb chops and place over sliced onion. Add garlic on top of lamb chops.
4. Cover pot aura with lid.
5. Select slow cook mode and cook on LOW for 6 hours.
6. Serve and enjoy.

Nutritional Value (Amount per Serving):

- Calories 225
- Fat 8.3 g
- Carbohydrates 3.7 g
- Sugar 1.3 g
- Protein 32.1 g
- Cholesterol 101 mg

Onion Pork Chops

Preparation Time: 10 minutes

Cooking Time: 6 hours

Serve: 4

Ingredients:

- 2 lbs pork chops, boneless
- 1/3 cup butter, sliced
- 1 onion, sliced
- 1/8 tsp red pepper flakes
- 1/4 tsp garlic powder
- 2 tbsp brown sugar
- 1 tbsp apple cider vinegar
- 2 tbsp Worcestershire sauce
- 1/4 tsp pepper
- 1/4 tsp salt

Directions:

1. Add pork chops into the cooking pot.
2. Pour remaining ingredients over pork chops into the cooking pot.
3. Cover pot aura with lid.
4. Select slow cook mode and cook on LOW for 6 hours.
5. Serve and enjoy.

Nutritional Value (Amount per Serving):

- Calories 899
- Fat 71.8 g
- Carbohydrates 8.8 g
- Sugar 7.1 g
- Protein 51.5 g
- Cholesterol 236 mg

Sweet Applesauce Pork Chops

Preparation Time: 10 minutes

Cooking Time: 4 hours

Serve: 4

Ingredients:

- 3 pork chops, boneless
- 1 1/2 cups applesauce
- 1 tsp Worcestershire sauce
- 1/3 cup BBQ sauce
- 1 tsp garlic powder
- 1/4 tsp black pepper
- 2 tbsp brown sugar
- 2 tbsp butter
- 1/4 tsp salt

Directions:

1. Add butter into the cooking pot and set pot aura on sauté mode.
2. Add pork chops into the pot and cook until brown from both the sides.
3. Add remaining ingredients over pork chops in a cooking pot and stir well.
4. Cover pot aura with lid.
5. Select slow cook mode and cook on HIGH for 4 hours.
6. Stir well and serve.

Nutritional Value (Amount per Serving):

- Calories 335
- Fat 20.8 g
- Carbohydrates 23.1 g
- Sugar 19.5 g
- Protein 13.8 g
- Cholesterol 67 mg

Beef Bean Casserole

Preparation Time: 10 minutes

Cooking Time: 8 hours

Serve: 6

Ingredients:

- 1 lb ground beef, browned and drained
- 1 can tomatoes with juice
- 1 can cream of mushroom soup
- 1 lb potatoes, sliced
- 1 cup cheddar cheese, shredded
- 1 can red kidney beans, drained
- 1 cup corn, drained
- 1/4 cup onion, diced
- 1/2 tsp pepper
- 1 tsp salt

Directions:

1. Add all ingredients except cheese in the cooking pot and stir well.
2. Cover pot aura with lid.
3. Select slow cook mode and cook on LOW for 8 hours.
4. Top with shredded cheese and cover and cook for 30 minutes more.
5. Serve and enjoy.

Nutritional Value (Amount per Serving):

- Calories 440
- Fat 14.6 g
- Carbohydrates 40.2 g
- Sugar 3.8 g
- Protein 37.6 g
- Cholesterol 87 mg

Butter Steak Bites

Preparation Time: 10 minutes

Cooking Time: 8 hours

Serve: 4

Ingredients:

- 3 lbs round steak, cut into 1-inch cubes
- 1/2 cup chicken broth
- 1/2 tsp black pepper
- 4 tbsp butter, sliced
- 1 tsp garlic powder
- 1 tbsp onion, minced
- 1/2 tsp salt

Directions:

1. Place meat cubes in the cooking pot and pour broth over the meat.
2. Sprinkle with garlic powder, onion, pepper, and salt.
3. Place butter slices on top of the meat.
4. Cover pot aura with lid.
5. Select slow cook mode and cook on LOW for 8 hours.
6. Serve and enjoy.

Nutritional Value (Amount per Serving):

- Calories 845
- Fat 44.4 g
- Carbohydrates 1 g
- Sugar 0.4 g
- Protein 103 g
- Cholesterol 320 mg

Apple Pork Loin

Preparation Time: 10 minutes

Cooking Time: 8 hours

Serve: 4

Ingredients:

- 1 1/2 lbs pork loin
- 3 apples, peeled, cored and chopped
- 1 cup apple cider
- 1 onion, sliced
- Pepper
- Salt

Directions:

1. Place pork in the cooking pot and top with sliced onion and apples.
2. Pour apple cider over pork onion and apple mixture.
3. Season with pepper and salt.
4. Cover pot aura with lid.
5. Select slow cook mode and cook on LOW for 8 hours.
6. Slice pork and serve.

Nutritional Value (Amount per Serving):

- Calories 539
- Fat 24.1 g
- Carbohydrates 32.9 g
- Sugar 25.3 g
- Protein 47.3 g
- Cholesterol 136 mg

Spicy Pork Chops

Preparation Time: 10 minutes

Cooking Time: 5 hours

Serve: 8

Ingredients:

- 4 lbs pork chops, boneless
- 1/4 cup cornstarch
- 1/2 cup brown sugar
- 1 tsp black pepper
- 1 tsp garlic, minced
- 1 tbsp red chili paste
- 1/4 cup soy sauce
- 1/2 cup ketchup
- 1/2 tsp kosher salt

Directions:

1. Add all ingredients except cornstarch and pork chop into the cooking pot and stir well.
2. Place pork chops in the cooking pot and stir well to coat.
3. Cover pot aura with lid.
4. Select slow cook mode and cook on LOW for 4 hours.
5. In a small bowl, whisk together little water and cornstarch and pour into the cooking pot.
6. Stir everything well and cook on low for 1 hour more.
7. Serve and enjoy.

Nutritional Value (Amount per Serving):

- Calories 802
- Fat 56.7 g
- Carbohydrates 18 g
- Sugar 12.9 g
- Protein 51.9 g
- Cholesterol 196 mg

Sweet & Sour Pork Tenderloin

Preparation Time: 10 minutes

Cooking Time: 6 hours

Serve: 4

Ingredients:

- 2 lbs lean pork tenderloin, cut into cubed
- 2 tbsp cornstarch
- 2 tomatoes, cut into sliced
- 1 small onion, sliced
- 1/4 cup apple cider vinegar
- 3 tbsp soy sauce
- 2 green bell peppers, cut into strips
- 1/4 cup brown sugar
- 1/4 tsp ground ginger

Directions:

1. Add all ingredients except bell pepper and tomatoes into the cooking pot and stir well.
2. Cover pot aura with lid.
3. Select slow cook mode and cook on LOW for 6 hours.
4. Stir in tomatoes and bell pepper.
5. Cover and cook on high for 10 minutes more
6. Stir well and serve over rice.

Nutritional Value (Amount per Serving):

- Calories 421
- Fat 8.3 g
- Carbohydrates 22.2 g
- Sugar 14.4 g
- Protein 61.5 g
- Cholesterol 166 mg

Orange Pork Roast

Preparation Time: 10 minutes

Cooking Time: 8 hours

Serve: 6

Ingredients:

- 4 lbs pork roast
- 1/4 cup orange marmalade
- 1/4 cup soy sauce
- 2 garlic cloves, minced
- 1 tbsp ketchup

Directions:

1. In a small bowl, mix together soy sauce, garlic, ketchup, and orange marmalade.
2. Brush soy sauce mixture all over pork roast.
3. Place pork roast in the cooking pot and pour the remaining sauce over pork roast.
4. Cover pot aura with lid.
5. Select slow cook mode and cook on LOW for 8 hours.
6. Slice and serve.

Nutritional Value (Amount per Serving):

- Calories 668
- Fat 28.5 g
- Carbohydrates 10.6 g
- Sugar 8.8 g
- Protein 87 g
- Cholesterol 260 mg

Asian Lamb Stew

Preparation Time: 10 minutes

Cooking Time: 4 hours

Serve: 4

Ingredients:

- 2 lbs lamb, boneless
- 2 tbsp vegetable oil
- 2 tsp ground cumin
- 2 tsp ground coriander
- 1 tsp ground turmeric
- 28 oz can tomato, crushed
- 1.5 tbsp maple syrup
- 2 medium onions, chopped
- 3 garlic cloves, chopped
- 1 tsp fresh ginger, grated
- 1 tsp dried mint
- 1 tsp garam masala
- 1 tsp red chili flakes
- 2 tsp salt

Directions:

1. Add oil, ginger, onion, and garlic into the cooking pot and set pot aura on sauté mode and sauté onion until softened.
2. Add lamb and sauté until browned.
3. Add remaining ingredients into the cooking and stir well.
4. Cover pot aura with lid.
5. Select slow cook mode and cook on HIGH for 4 hours.
6. Serve and enjoy.

Nutritional Value (Amount per Serving):

- Calories 577
- Fat 23.8 g
- Carbohydrates 22.2 g
- Sugar 13.6 g
- Protein 66.5 g
- Cholesterol 204 mg

Spicy Green Chili Beef

Preparation Time: 10 minutes

Cooking Time: 8 hours

Serve: 8

Ingredients:

- 2 lbs beef chuck roast
- 1 tsp chili powder
- 4 fresh Anaheim Chile peppers, chopped
- 1 onion, sliced
- 1 tsp ground cumin
- 1 1/2 tsp salt

Directions:

1. Add the meat into the cooking pot then mix together the remaining ingredients and pour over the meat.
2. Cover pot aura with lid.
3. Select slow cook mode and cook on LOW for 8 hours.
4. Remove meat from pot and shred using a fork.
5. Return shredded meat into the pot and stir well.
6. Serve and enjoy.

Nutritional Value (Amount per Serving):

- Calories 419
- Fat 31.7 g
- Carbohydrates 1.6 g
- Sugar 0.6 g
- Protein 29.9 g
- Cholesterol 117 mg

Thyme Garlic Lamb Chops

Preparation Time: 10 minutes

Cooking Time: 6 hours

Serve: 2

Ingredients:

- 2 lamb shoulder chops, bone-in
- 1/2 cup red wine
- 1 cup beef broth
- 1/4 cup fresh thyme
- 1 tsp garlic paste
- Pepper
- Salt

Directions:

1. Add all ingredients into the cooking pot and stir well.
2. Cover pot aura with lid.
3. Select slow cook mode and cook on LOW for 6 hours.
4. Stir well and serve.

Nutritional Value (Amount per Serving):

- Calories 237
- Fat 7.1 g
- Carbohydrates 6.4 g
- Sugar 0.9 g
- Protein 26.1 g
- Cholesterol 75 mg

Creamy Mushroom Pork Chops

Preparation Time: 10 minutes

Cooking Time: 6 hours

Serve: 4

Ingredients:

- 4 pork chops, bone-in
- 1 can cream of mushroom soup
- 2 cups onion, chopped
- 1 tsp garlic, minced
- 16 oz mushrooms, sliced
- 1 can cream of chicken soup
- 1/2 tsp black pepper

Directions:

1. Add chopped onion into the cooking pot.
2. Place pork chops on top of onion in the cooking pot.
3. In a bowl, mix together the remaining ingredients and pour over pork chops.
4. Cover pot aura with lid.
5. Select slow cook mode and cook on LOW for 6 hours.
6. Serve over rice and enjoy.

Nutritional Value (Amount per Serving):

- Calories 436
- Fat 28.9 g
- Carbohydrates 19.8 g
- Sugar 5.9 g
- Protein 25.2 g
- Cholesterol 75 mg

Slow Cook Beef Brisket

Preparation Time: 10 minutes

Cooking Time: 8 hours

Serve: 8

Ingredients:

- 3 lbs beef brisket

For sauce:

- 1/2 tsp parsley
- 1/4 cup dried onion flakes
- 1/2 cup beef broth
- 28 oz tomatoes, diced
- 2 tbsp garlic salt
- 1/8 tsp pepper
- 1/8 tsp paprika
- 1/4 tsp onion powder

Directions:

1. Add the meat into the cooking pot then mix together the remaining ingredients and pour over the meat.
2. Cover pot aura with lid.
3. Select slow cook mode and cook on LOW for 8 hours.
4. Remove meat from pot and shred using a fork.
5. Return shredded meat into the pot and stir well.
6. Serve and enjoy.

Nutritional Value (Amount per Serving):

- Calories 350
- Fat 10.9 g
- Carbohydrates 7 g
- Sugar 3.8 g
- Protein 53.3 g
- Cholesterol 152 mg

Balsamic Lamb Chops

Preparation Time: 10 minutes

Cooking Time: 6 hours

Serve: 6

Ingredients:

- 3.5 lbs lamb chops, trimmed off
- 2 tbsp balsamic vinegar
- 4 garlic cloves, minced
- 1 large onion, sliced
- 1/2 tsp ground black pepper
- 2 tbsp rosemary
- 1/2 tsp salt

Directions:

1. Add onion into the cooking pot.
2. Place lamb chops on top of onions, then add rosemary, vinegar, garlic, pepper, and salt.
3. Cover pot aura with lid.
4. Select slow cook mode and cook on LOW for 6 hours.
5. Serve and enjoy.

Nutritional Value (Amount per Serving):

- Calories 510
- Fat 19.6 g
- Carbohydrates 3.9 g
- Sugar 1.1 g
- Protein 74.8 g
- Cholesterol 238 mg

Cheesy Taco Casserole

Preparation Time: 10 minutes

Cooking Time: 2 hours

Serve: 10

Ingredients:

- 1 lb ground beef
- 1/2 package taco seasoning
- 1 can tomatoes, diced
- 1 can black beans, drained
- 8 oz cheddar cheese, shredded
- 2 cups rice, cooked
- 1 cup of corn
- 1/2 onion, chopped

Directions:

1. Add the meat into the cooking pot and set pot aura on sauté mode and cook meat until brown.
2. Remove meat from the cooking pot.
3. Add in onions, corn, beans, tomatoes, and taco seasoning. Stir to combine and set aside.
4. Spread rice in the bottom of the cooking pot then layer with meat mixture and top with shredded cheese.
5. Cover pot aura with lid.
6. Select slow cook mode and cook on HIGH for 2 hours.
7. Serve and enjoy.

Nutritional Value (Amount per Serving):

- Calories 414
- Fat 12.1 g
- Carbohydrates 47.4 g
- Sugar 1.8 g
- Protein 28 g
- Cholesterol 67 mg

Beef Stew

Preparation Time: 10 minutes

Cooking Time: 8 hours

Serve: 4

Ingredients:

- 1 lb beef stew meat
- 1 tbsp curry powder
- 1 fresh jalapeno pepper, diced
- 1 tsp fresh ginger, chopped
- 2 garlic cloves, minced
- 1 tbsp vegetable oil
- 1 cup beef broth
- 1 onion, sliced
- 14 oz can tomato, diced
- Pepper
- Salt

Directions:

1. Add oil and meat into the cooking pot and set pot aura on sauté mode. Sauté meat until brown.
2. Pour remaining ingredients into the cooking pot.
3. Cover pot aura with lid.
4. Select slow cook mode and cook on LOW for 8 hours.
5. Serve and enjoy.

Nutritional Value (Amount per Serving):

- Calories 293
- Fat 11.1 g
- Carbohydrates 9.8 g
- Sugar 4.9 g
- Protein 37.2 g
- Cholesterol 101 mg

Chapter 7: Fish & Seafood

Caribbean Shrimp

Preparation Time: 10 minutes

Cooking Time: 2 hours

Serve: 4

Ingredients:

- 12 oz frozen shrimp, thawed
- 2 cups cooked rice
- 1/2 cup tomatoes, diced
- 1 cup frozen peas, thawed
- 1/2 tsp dried oregano
- 1 tsp chili powder
- 1/2 tsp garlic powder
- 1/2 cup chicken broth

Directions:

1. Add shrimp, oregano, chili powder, garlic powder, and broth into the cooking pot and stir well.
2. Cover pot aura with lid.
3. Select slow cook mode and cook on LOW for 2 hours.
4. Stir in rice, tomatoes, and peas. Cover and let it sit for 10 minutes.
5. Stir well and serve.

Nutritional Value (Amount per Serving):

- Calories 472
- Fat 2.6 g
- Carbohydrates 82.1 g
- Sugar 2.8 g
- Protein 27 g
- Cholesterol 128 mg

Shrimp Casserole

Preparation Time: 10 minutes

Cooking Time: 8 hours

Serve: 6

Ingredients:

- 1 1/2 lbs frozen shrimp, peeled and deveined
- 1 can Rotel
- 1 can cream of chicken soup
- 1 can cream of celery soup
- 1 cup chicken broth
- 2 cups rice, uncooked
- 1 tsp dried parsley
- 1 tbsp garlic powder
- 1 yellow bell pepper, chopped
- 1 red bell pepper, chopped
- 1 onion, chopped
- 1 tsp pepper
- 1 tsp salt

Directions:

1. Add all ingredients into the cooking pot and stir well.
2. Cover pot aura with lid.
3. Select slow cook mode and cook on LOW for 8 hours.
4. Stir well and serve.

Nutritional Value (Amount per Serving):

- Calories 495
- Fat 8.2 g
- Carbohydrates 70.7 g
- Sugar 4.6 g
- Protein 32.3 g
- Cholesterol 180 mg

Shrimp Pasta

Preparation Time: 10 minutes

Cooking Time: 1 hour 30 minutes

Serve: 4

Ingredients:

- 1 lb shrimp, peeled and deveined
- 1/4 cup fresh parsley, minced
- 1 cup wheat orzo pasta
- 1 tbsp butter
- 1/2 cup dry white wine
- 4 cups vegetable broth
- 2 tsp garlic, minced
- Pepper
- Salt

Directions:

1. Add all ingredients into the cooking pot and stir well.
2. Cover pot aura with lid.
3. Select slow cook mode and cook on LOW for 1 1/2 hours.
4. Stir well and serve.

Nutritional Value (Amount per Serving):

- Calories 292
- Fat 7.1 g
- Carbohydrates 16.2 g
- Sugar 2.5 g
- Protein 33.4 g
- Cholesterol 249 mg

Thai Shrimp Rice

Preparation Time: 10 minutes

Cooking Time: 3 hours 30 minutes

Serve: 6

Ingredients:

- 1 lb shrimp, peeled, deveined, & cooked
- 1/2 cup snow peas, cut into thin strips
- 2 cups white rice
- 1/4 cup raisins
- 1/4 cup flaked coconut
- 1 carrot, shredded
- 1 bell pepper, diced
- 1 onion, chopped
- 2 tbsp garlic, minced
- 2 lime juice
- 3/4 tsp cayenne
- 1 tsp cumin
- 1 tsp ground coriander
- 1 cup of water
- 28 oz chicken broth
- 1 tsp salt

Directions:

1. Add all ingredients except coconut, snow peas, and shrimp into the cooking pot and stir well.
2. Cover pot aura with lid.
3. Select slow cook mode and cook on LOW for 3 hours.
4. Stir in snow peas and shrimp, cover and cook on LOW for 30 minutes more.
5. Top with flaked coconut and serve.

Nutritional Value (Amount per Serving):

- Calories 399
- Fat 3.8 g
- Carbohydrates 63.8 g
- Sugar 7.4 g
- Protein 25.8 g
- Cholesterol 159 mg

Creamy Curried Shrimp

Preparation Time: 10 minutes

Cooking Time: 4 hours 10 minutes

Serve: 4

Ingredients:

- 2 cups shrimp, cooked
- 1 small onion, chopped
- 10 oz can cream of mushroom soup
- 1 cup sour cream
- 1 tsp curry powder

Directions:

1. Add all ingredients except cream into the cooking pot and stir well.
2. Cover pot aura with lid.
3. Select slow cook mode and cook on LOW for 4 hours.
4. Stir in cream and serve.

Nutritional Value (Amount per Serving):

- Calories 219
- Fat 14.1 g
- Carbohydrates 10.4 g
- Sugar 2.4 g
- Protein 12.6 g
- Cholesterol 117 mg

Shrimp Scallop Stew

Preparation Time: 10 minutes

Cooking Time: 4 hours 30 minutes

Serve: 6

Ingredients:

- 1 lb large shrimp
- 1/8 tsp cayenne pepper
- 1 lb scallops
- 1 medium onion, chopped
- 1 lb potatoes, cut into pieces
- 2 garlic cloves, minced
- 4 cups vegetable broth
- 1/4 tsp red chili flakes
- 1 tsp oregano, dried
- 1 tsp basil, dried
- 1 tsp thyme, dried
- 1 tbsp tomato paste
- 28 oz can tomato, crushed
- 1/4 tsp Pepper
- 1/2 tsp salt

Directions:

1. Add all ingredients except shrimp and scallop into the cooking pot and stir well.
2. Cover pot aura with lid.
3. Select slow cook mode and cook on LOW for 4 hours.
4. Add shrimp and scallops and stir well, cover, and cook for 30 minutes more.
5. Stir well and serve.

Nutritional Value (Amount per Serving):

- Calories 246
- Fat 1.7 g
- Carbohydrates 25.3 g
- Sugar 7 g
- Protein 33 g
- Cholesterol 133 mg

Shrimp Curry

Preparation Time: 10 minutes

Cooking Time: 2 hours 15 minutes

Serve: 4

Ingredients:

- 1 lb shrimp, with shells
- 1/2 cup red curry sauce
- 15 oz water
- 30 oz coconut milk

Directions:

1. Add all ingredients except shrimp into the cooking pot and stir well.
2. Cover pot aura with lid.
3. Select slow cook mode and cook on HIGH for 2 hours.
4. Add shrimp and stir well, cover, and cook for 15 minutes more.
5. Stir well and serve.

Nutritional Value (Amount per Serving):

- Calories 634
- Fat 53.4 g
- Carbohydrates 14.4 g
- Sugar 7.5 g
- Protein 30.7 g
- Cholesterol 239 mg

Shrimp Grits

Preparation Time: 10 minutes

Cooking Time: 3 hours 40 minutes

Serve: 8

Ingredients:

- 2 lbs raw shrimp
- 1 cup cheddar cheese, shredded
- 1 tsp dried thyme
- 1 tbsp onion powder
- 1 tbsp garlic powder
- 1 1/2 cups grits
- 6 cups chicken broth
- 1/2 tsp hot sauce
- 1/2 cup parmesan cheese, grated
- 4 oz cream cheese
- Pepper
- Salt

Directions:

1. Add all ingredients except shrimp into the cooking pot and stir well.
2. Cover pot aura with lid.
3. Select slow cook mode and cook on LOW for 3 hours.
4. Add shrimp and stir well, cover, and cook on LOW for 30 minutes more.
5. Stir well and serve.

Nutritional Value (Amount per Serving):

- Calories 322
- Fat 14.4 g
- Carbohydrates 9.2 g
- Sugar 1.8 g
- Protein 37.1 g
- Cholesterol 274 mg

Louisiana Shrimp

Preparation Time: 10 minutes

Cooking Time: 1 hour 30 minutes

Serve: 4

Ingredients:

- 1 lb shrimp, deveined
- 1 tsp garlic, minced
- 1 tsp old bay seasoning
- 1 tbsp Worcestershire sauce
- 1 lemon juice
- 1/2 cup butter, sliced
- 1/2 tsp pepper
- 1/2 tsp salt

Directions:

1. Add all ingredients into the cooking pot and stir well.
2. Cover pot aura with lid.
3. Select slow cook mode and cook on HIGH for 1 1/2 hours.
4. Serve and enjoy.

Nutritional Value (Amount per Serving):

- Calories 343
- Fat 25 g
- Carbohydrates 2.4 g
- Sugar 0.3 g
- Protein 26.2 g
- Cholesterol 300 mg

Asian Salmon

Preparation Time: 10 minutes

Cooking Time: 1 hour

Serve: 6

Ingredients:

- 6 salmon fillets
- 1/8 cup lime juice
- 1/2 cup maple syrup
- 1 tsp ginger, minced
- 2 tsp garlic, crushed
- 1/4 cup soy sauce

Directions:

1. Place salmon fillets in the cooking pot.
2. In a bowl, mix together the remaining ingredients and pour over salmon fillets.
3. Cover pot aura with lid.
4. Select slow cook mode and cook on HIGH for 1 hour.
5. Serve and enjoy.

Nutritional Value (Amount per Serving):

- Calories 312
- Fat 11.1 g
- Carbohydrates 19 g
- Sugar 15.8 g
- Protein 35.3 g
- Cholesterol 78 mg

Chapter 8: Snacks & Appetizers

Spicy Chili Queso Dip

Preparation Time: 10 minutes

Cooking Time: 2 hours

Serve: 10

Ingredients:

- 32 oz Velveeta cheese, chop into chunks
- 1/2 tsp cayenne pepper
- 2 tbsp cumin
- 2 tbsp paprika
- 3 tbsp chili powder
- 6 tbsp lime juice
- 2 cups of milk
- 30 oz can no bean chili

Directions:

1. Add all ingredients into the cooking pot and stir well.
2. Cover pot aura with lid.
3. Select slow cook mode and cook on LOW for 2 hours. Stir halfway through.
4. Stir well and serve.

Nutritional Value (Amount per Serving):

- Calories 401
- Fat 26 g
- Carbohydrates 27 g
- Sugar 10.4 g
- Protein 23.5 g
- Cholesterol 83 mg

Cheesy Onion Dip

Preparation Time: 10 minutes

Cooking Time: 4 hours 30 minutes

Serve: 12

Ingredients:

- 4 onions, sliced
- 1/2 cup mozzarella cheese
- 8 oz sour cream
- 2 tbsp olive oil
- 2 tbsp butter
- Pepper
- Salt

Directions:

1. Add oil, butter, and onions into the cooking pot and stir well.
2. Cover pot aura with lid.
3. Select slow cook mode and cook on HIGH for 4 hours.
4. Transfer onion mixture to the blender with sour cream, pepper, and salt and blend until creamy.
5. Return onion dip into the cooking pot.
6. Add mozzarella cheese and stir well.
7. Cover pot aura with lid.
8. Select slow cook mode and cook on LOW for 30 minutes.
9. Stir well and serve.

Nutritional Value (Amount per Serving):

- Calories 95
- Fat 8.5 g
- Carbohydrates 4.3 g
- Sugar 1.6 g
- Protein 1.4 g
- Cholesterol 14 mg

Perfect Sausage Dip

Preparation Time: 10 minutes

Cooking Time: 1 hour 30 minutes

Serve: 6

Ingredients:

- 12 oz sausage, cooked
- 1/2 tsp onion powder
- 1 tsp garlic, minced
- 24 oz cream cheese
- 10 oz Rotel
- 1/2 tsp salt

Directions:

1. Add all ingredients into the cooking pot and stir well.
2. Cover pot aura with lid.
3. Select slow cook mode and cook on HIGH for 1 1/2 hours.
4. Stir well and serve.

Nutritional Value (Amount per Serving):

- Calories 767
- Fat 56.5 g
- Carbohydrates 38.8 g
- Sugar 2 g
- Protein 25.5 g
- Cholesterol 172 mg

Cheesy Artichoke Dip

Preparation Time: 10 minutes

Cooking Time: 2 hours

Serve: 6

Ingredients:

- 14 oz can artichokes, drained & chopped
- 1 lb spinach, stems removed
- 1/4 tsp black pepper
- 1 garlic cloves, minced
- 1/4 cup parmesan cheese, grated
- 1/2 lb cream cheese, cubed
- 1 cup mozzarella cheese, shredded

Directions:

1. Add all ingredients into the cooking pot and stir well.
2. Cover pot aura with lid.
3. Select slow cook mode and cook on HIGH for 2 hours.
4. Stir well and serve.

Nutritional Value (Amount per Serving):

- Calories 230
- Fat 16.6 g
- Carbohydrates 12.4 g
- Sugar 1.1 g
- Protein 11.4 g
- Cholesterol 51 mg

Chili Cheese Dip

Preparation Time: 10 minutes

Cooking Time: 3 hours

Serve: 12

Ingredients:

- 1 lb ground beef
- 4 oz cream cheese, cubed & softened
- 2 1/2 cups cheddar cheese, shredded
- 1 tsp cumin
- 1 1/2 tsp chili powder
- 1 1/2 tsp garlic powder
- 4 oz can green chilies, chopped
- 1 cup chicken broth
- 1 1/2 cup salsa
- 15 oz can chili beans
- 3 tbsp all-purpose flour
- 1 small onion, chopped

Directions:

1. Set pot aura on sauté mode.
2. Add ground beef and onion into the cooking pot and sauté until meat is no longer pink.
3. Add flour and stir well to combine.
4. Add remaining ingredients and stir everything well.
5. Cover pot aura with lid.
6. Select slow cook mode and cook on LOW for 3 hours.
7. Stir well and serve.

Nutritional Value (Amount per Serving):

- Calories 584
- Fat 16.3 g
- Carbohydrates 53.1 g
- Sugar 17.1 g
- Protein 41.4 g
- Cholesterol 69 mg

Mexican Quinoa Dip

Preparation Time: 10 minutes

Cooking Time: 3 hours

Serve: 12

Ingredients:

- 1 cup quinoa, uncooked
- 2 cups salsa
- 2 cups corn kernels
- 2 cups vegetable broth
- 1/2 tsp paprika
- 1/2 tsp ground cumin
- 1/2 tsp black pepper
- 1 tsp oregano
- 1 tsp garlic, minced
- 1 tbsp lime juice
- 1 1/2 tbsp chili powder
- 1 cup bell pepper, chopped
- 1 cup black beans
- 1/4 tsp salt

Directions:

1. Add all ingredients into the cooking pot and stir well.
2. Cover pot aura with lid.
3. Select slow cook mode and cook on HIGH for 3 hours.
4. Stir well and serve.

Nutritional Value (Amount per Serving):

- Calories 156
- Fat 1.9 g
- Carbohydrates 28.7 g
- Sugar 3.3 g
- Protein 8.1 g
- Cholesterol 0 mg

Mexican Dip

Preparation Time: 10 minutes

Cooking Time: 1 hour

Serve: 6

Ingredients:

- 1 cup tomatoes with green chilies
- 8 oz Velveeta cheese, cut into cube
- 1 tsp taco seasoning

Directions:

1. Add cheese into the cooking pot.
2. Select slow cook mode and cook on LOW for 30 minutes. Stir occasionally.
3. Add taco seasoning and tomatoes with green chilies and stir well.
4. Cover pot aura with lid.
5. Select slow cook mode and cook on LOW for 30 minutes.
6. Stir well and serve.

Nutritional Value (Amount per Serving):

- Calories 176
- Fat 11.6 g
- Carbohydrates 9.9 g
- Sugar 2.7 g
- Protein 10.5 g
- Cholesterol 36 mg

Corn Jalapeno Popper Dip

Preparation Time: 10 minutes

Cooking Time: 2 hours

Serve: 8

Ingredients:

- 2 jalapeno peppers, seeded & diced
- 45 oz can fire-roasted corn, drained
- 1/2 lb bacon, cooked & chopped
- 8 oz cream cheese, cubed
- 1 cup Mexican cheese blend, shredded
- 1/2 cup sour cream
- Pepper
- Salt

Directions:

1. Add all ingredients except cream cheese and bacon into the cooking pot and stir well.
2. Add cream cheese on top of corn mixture into the cooking pot.
3. Cover pot aura with lid.
4. Select slow cook mode and cook on LOW for 2 hours.
5. Top with bacon and serve.

Nutritional Value (Amount per Serving):

- Calories 481
- Fat 26.3 g
- Carbohydrates 41.7 g
- Sugar 5 g
- Protein 23.2 g
- Cholesterol 70 mg

Baked Jalapeno Poppers

Preparation Time: 10 minutes

Cooking Time: 20 minutes

Serve: 20

Ingredients:

- 10 jalapeno peppers, sliced in half & scoop out insides
- 1 tsp cumin
- 1 tsp garlic powder
- 1 tsp chili powder
- 8 oz cheddar cheese, shredded
- 8 oz cream cheese, softened
- Pepper
- salt

Directions:

1. In a bowl, mix together cream cheese, cheddar cheese, chili powder, garlic powder, cumin, pepper, and salt.
2. Stuff cream cheese mixture into each jalapeno half.
3. Place stuff jalapeno half into the cooking pot.
4. Cover pot aura with lid.
5. Select bake mode then set the temperature to 350 F and timer for 20 minutes.
6. Serve and enjoy.

Nutritional Value (Amount per Serving):

- Calories 90
- Fat 7.9 g
- Carbohydrates 1.2 g
- Sugar 0.4 g
- Protein 3.8 g
- Cholesterol 24 mg

Italian Tomato Dip

Preparation Time: 10 minutes

Cooking Time: 1 hour

Serve: 20

Ingredients:

- 1/4 cup sun-dried tomatoes
- 1 tbsp mayonnaise
- 8 oz cream cheese
- 3 garlic cloves
- 1/4 tsp white pepper
- 1 tsp pine nuts, toasted
- 3/4 oz fresh basil

Directions:

1. Add all ingredients into the blender and blend until smooth.
2. Pour blended mixture into the cooking pot.
3. Cover pot aura with lid.
4. Select slow cook mode and cook on LOW for 1 hour.
5. Stir well and serve.

Nutritional Value (Amount per Serving):

- Calories 45
- Fat 4.3 g
- Carbohydrates 0.8 g
- Sugar 0.1 g
- Protein 1 g
- Cholesterol 13 mg

Chapter 9: Desserts

Pineapple Tapioca

Preparation Time: 10 minutes

Cooking Time: 3 hours

Serve: 6

Ingredients:

- 15 oz can pineapple, crushed and undrained
- 2 1/2 cups pineapple juice
- 2 1/2 cups water
- 3/4 cup sugar
- 1/2 cup tapioca pearl

Directions:

1. Add all ingredients except pineapple into the cooking pot and stir well.
2. Cover pot aura with lid.
3. Select slow cook mode and cook on HIGH for 3 hours.
4. Stir in pineapple.
5. Serve chilled and enjoy.

Nutritional Value (Amount per Serving):

- Calories 237
- Fat 0.2 g
- Carbohydrates 60.8 g
- Sugar 46.1 g
- Protein 0.7 g
- Cholesterol 0 mg

Choco Rice Pudding

Preparation Time: 10 minutes

Cooking Time: 2 hours 30 minutes

Serve: 8

Ingredients:

- 2 cups sticky rice, rinsed & drained
- 1/2 cup chocolate chips
- 1/2 cup brown sugar
- 14 oz coconut milk
- 12 oz can evaporate milk
- 3 cups of water
- 1/2 cup cocoa powder

Directions:

1. Add rice, water, and cocoa powder into the cooking pot and stir well.
2. Cover pot aura with lid.
3. Select slow cook mode and cook on HIGH for 2 hours.
4. Add remaining ingredients and stir everything well, cover, and cook for 30 minutes more.
5. Serve and enjoy.

Nutritional Value (Amount per Serving):

- Calories 327
- Fat 19.4 g
- Carbohydrates 36.4 g
- Sugar 16 g
- Protein 6.7 g
- Cholesterol 15 mg

Walnut Peanut Butter Cake

Preparation Time: 10 minutes

Cooking Time: 2 hours 30 minutes

Serve: 10

Ingredients:

- 2 eggs
- 1/2 cup water
- 2 cups chocolate cake mix
- 1/2 cup walnuts, chopped
- 6 tbsp peanut butter

Directions:

1. Add all ingredients into the large bowl and beat for 2 minutes.
2. Line pot aura cooking pot with parchment paper.
3. Pour batter into the cooking pot.
4. Cover pot aura with lid.
5. Select slow cook mode and cook on HIGH for 2 1/2 hours.
6. Cut into pieces and serve.

Nutritional Value (Amount per Serving):

- Calories 236
- Fat 14.1 g
- Carbohydrates 24.5 g
- Sugar 12.5 g
- Protein 6.8 g
- Cholesterol 33 mg

Easy Peach Cobbler Cake

Preparation Time: 10 minutes

Cooking Time: 45 minutes

Serve: 8

Ingredients:

- 3/4 cup butter, cut into pieces
- 1 oz yellow cake mix
- 20 oz can pineapples, crushed
- 21 oz can peach pie filling

Directions:

1. Pour crushed pineapples and peach pie filling into the cooking pot and spread evenly.
2. Sprinkle cake mix on top of pineapple mixture then places butter pieces on top of the cake mix.
3. Cover pot aura with lid.
4. Select Bake mode and set the temperature to 350 F and time for 45 minutes.
5. Serve with vanilla ice cream.

Nutritional Value (Amount per Serving):

- Calories 175
- Fat 2.3 g
- Carbohydrates 38.5 g
- Sugar 21.1 g
- Protein 1.2 g
- Cholesterol 0 mg

Baked Peaches

Preparation Time: 10 minutes

Cooking Time: 10 minutes

Serve: 6

Ingredients:

- 3 ripe peaches, slice in half & remove the pit
- 1/4 tsp cinnamon
- 2 tbsp brown sugar
- 1 tbsp butter

Directions:

1. Mix together butter, brown sugar, and cinnamon and place in the middle of each peach piece.
2. Place peaches in the cooking pot.
3. Cover pot aura with lid.
4. Select Bake mode and set the temperature to 375 F and time for 10 minutes.
5. Serve and enjoy.

Nutritional Value (Amount per Serving):

- Calories 58
- Fat 2.1 g
- Carbohydrates 10 g
- Sugar 9.9 g
- Protein 0.7 g
- Cholesterol 5 mg

Tasty Cherry Cobbler

Preparation Time: 10 minutes

Cooking Time: 2 hours

Serve: 6

Ingredients:

- 1/2 cup butter, cut into pieces
- 1 box cake mix
- 30 oz can cherry pie filling

Directions:

1. Add cherry pie filling into the cooking pot then sprinkle cake mix over cherry pie filling evenly.
2. Spread butter pieces on top of the cake mix.
3. Cover pot aura with lid.
4. Select slow cook mode and cook on HIGH for 2 hours.
5. Serve and enjoy.

Nutritional Value (Amount per Serving):

- Calories 671
- Fat 25 g
- Carbohydrates 107.8 g
- Sugar 47.6 g
- Protein 4.6 g
- Cholesterol 41 mg

Maple Pears

Preparation Time: 10 minutes

Cooking Time: 4 hours

Serve: 4

Ingredients:

- 4 ripe pears, peel, core, and cut the bottom
- 1/4 cup maple syrup
- 2 cups orange juice
- 1 tbsp ginger, sliced
- 1 cinnamon stick
- 5 cardamom pods

Directions:

1. Place pears into the cooking pot.
2. Mix together the remaining ingredients and pour over pears into the cooking pot.
3. Cover pot aura with lid.
4. Select slow cook mode and cook on LOW for 4 hours.
5. Serve warm and enjoy.

Nutritional Value (Amount per Serving):

- Calories 242
- Fat 0.8 g
- Carbohydrates 61.1 g
- Sugar 42.6 g
- Protein 2 g
- Cholesterol 0 mg

Delicious Apple Crisp

Preparation Time: 10 minutes

Cooking Time: 3 hours

Serve: 8

Ingredients:

- 2 lbs apples, peeled & sliced
- 1/2 cup butter
- 1/4 tsp ground nutmeg
- 1/2 tsp ground cinnamon
- 2/3 cup brown sugar
- 2/3 cup flour
- 2/3 cup old-fashioned oats

Directions:

1. Add sliced apples into the cooking pot.
2. In a mixing bowl, mix together flour, nutmeg, cinnamon, sugar, and oats.
3. Add butter into the flour mixture and mix until mixture is crumbly.
4. Sprinkle flour mixture over sliced apples.
5. Cover pot aura with lid.
6. Select slow cook mode and cook on HIGH for 2-3 hours.
7. Top with vanilla ice-cream and serve.

Nutritional Value (Amount per Serving):

- Calories 251
- Fat 12.1 g
- Carbohydrates 33.5 g
- Sugar 11.9 g
- Protein 2.1 g
- Cholesterol 31 mg

Cocoa Almond Butter Brownies

Preparation Time: 10 minutes

Cooking Time: 20 minutes

Serve: 4

Ingredients:

- 1/2 cup almond butter, melted
- 1 cup bananas, overripe
- 1 scoop protein powder
- 2 tbsp cocoa powder

Directions:

1. Line pot aura cooking pot with parchment paper.
2. Add all ingredients into the blender and blend until smooth.
3. Pour batter into the cooking pot.
4. Cover pot aura with lid.
5. Select bake mode then set the temperature to 350 F and timer for 20 minutes.
6. Slice and serve.

Nutritional Value (Amount per Serving):

- Calories 82
- Fat 2.1 g
- Carbohydrates 11.4 g
- Sugar 5 g
- Protein 6.9 g
- Cholesterol 16 mg

Chocolate Almond Fudge

Preparation Time: 10 minutes

Cooking Time: 6 hours

Serve: 30

Ingredients:

- 8 oz chocolate chips
- 1/2 cup milk
- 2 tbsp almonds, sliced
- 2 tbsp swerve
- 1 tbsp butter, melted

Directions:

1. Add chocolate chips, milk, butter, and swerve into the cooking pot and stir well.
2. Cover pot aura with lid.
3. Select slow cook mode and cook on LOW for 2 hours.
4. Add almonds and stir fudge until smooth.
5. Pour fudge mixture into the greased baking dish and spread evenly.
6. Place baking dish in the refrigerator until the fudge set.
7. Cut into squares and serve.

Nutritional Value (Amount per Serving):

- Calories 49
- Fat 2.9 g
- Carbohydrates 4.9 g
- Sugar 4.1 g
- Protein 0.8 g
- Cholesterol 3 mg

Conclusion

With the Cuisinart Multi-Cooker Cookbook, you'll learn a revolutionary new cooking method that saves you time and stress while making dinner for the family. This cookbook is more than just your average recipe book, though. Inside these pages, you'll find a plethora of beginner and advanced recipes to make in Cuisinart Multi-Cooker.

No matter what type of food you're craving, we guarantee there's a recipe to satisfy that craving in this cookbook!

Printed in the USA
CPSIA information can be obtained
at www.ICGtesting.com
LVHW080028291023
762209LV00008B/202